HOLT
1
FRENCH

Allez, viens!

Alternative Assessment Guide

HOLT, RINEHART AND WINSTON

A Harcourt Classroom Education Company

Austin · New York · Orlando · Atlanta · San Francisco · Boston · Dallas · Toronto · London

Contributing Writer

Portfolio Activities

Catharine Dallas Purdy
Austin Community College
Austin, TX

Cover Photo/Illustration Credits
Group of students: Marty Granger/HRW Photo; paint brushes: Image Copyright © 1999 Photodisc, Inc.

ALLEZ, VIENS! is a trademark licensed to Holt, Rinehart and Winston, registered in the United States of America and/or other jurisdictions.

Printed in the United States of America

ISBN 0-03-065559-5

3   4   5   6   7   066   05   04   03

Contents

To the Teacher

Individual students have individual needs and ways of learning, and progress at different rates in the development of their oral and written skills. The *Alternative Assessment Guide* is designed to accommodate those differences, and to offer opportunities for all students to be evaluated in the most favorable light possible and under circumstances that enable them to succeed.

The *Alternative Assessment Guide* contains information and suggestions for assessing student progress in three ways that go beyond the standard quizzes and tests: portfolio assessment, performance assessment, and CD-ROM assessment. Each section of the guide contains some general information and specific, chapter-related suggestions for incorporating each type of assessment into your instructional plan.

Portfolio Assessment

Student portfolios are of great benefit to foreign language students and teachers alike because they provide documentation of a student's efforts, progress, and achievements over a given period of time. In addition, students can receive both positive feedback and constructive criticism by sharing their portfolios with teachers, family, and peers. The opportunity for self-reflection provided by using a portfolio encourages students to participate in their learning in a positive way, thus fostering pride, ownership, and self-esteem.

This guide includes a variety of materials that will help you implement and assess student portfolios. The written and oral activity evaluation forms, student and teacher checklists, peer editing rubric, and portfolio evaluation sheets included here are designed for use with student portfolios, or for independent use, as part of any assessment program.

Determining a Purpose

The first step in implementing the portfolios in your classroom is to determine the purpose for which they will be used. You can use portfolios to assess individual students' growth and progress, to make students active in the assessment process, to provide evidence and documentation of students' work for more effective communication with parents, or to evaluate an instructional program of curriculum. Both the contents of the portfolio and the manner in which it is to be evaluated will depend directly on the purpose(s) the portfolio is to serve. Before including any work in their portfolios, students should understand the purpose of the portfolio and the criteria by which their work will be evaluated.

Setting up the Portfolios

While portfolios can be used to meet a variety of objectives, they are especially useful tools for assessing written and oral work. Written items can be in a variety of formats including lists, posters, personal correspondence, poems, stories, articles, and essays, depending on the level and needs of the students. Oral items, such as conversations, interviews, commercials, and skits, may be recorded on audio- or videocassette for incorporation into the portfolio. Whatever the format, both written and oral work can include evidence of the developmental process, such as notes from brainstorming, outlines, early drafts, or scripts, as well as the finished product.

Each student can be responsible for keeping the materials selected for his or her portfolio. Encourage students to personalize the presentation of their portfolios and to keep in mind that their portfolios may include audiocassettes, videocassettes, or diskettes, as well as papers.

Selecting Materials for the Portfolio

There are several ways you and your students can select materials to include in portfolios. The portfolio should not be seen as a repository for all student work. Work to be included should be selected on the basis of the portfolio's purpose and evaluation criteria to be used.

Student Selection   Many teachers prefer to let students choose samples of their best work to include in their portfolios. Early in the year, you may tell students how many written and oral items to include in their portfolios (for example, one written item and one oral item per chapter) and allow students the freedom to choose those pieces that they feel best represent their ability in the language. In this case, the written and oral portfolio items suggested in this guide would be treated as any other writing or speaking activities, and students would have the option to include these in their portfolios. This option empowers students by allowing them to decide what to include in their portfolios. The feeling of ownership of the portfolio is likely to increase as their involvement at the decision-making level increases.

Teacher-Directed Selection   Some teachers prefer to maintain portfolios that contain students' responses to specific prompts or activities. The oral and written portfolio items suggested in this guide, or other writing or speaking activities of your choice, could be assigned specifically for inclusion in the portfolio. This type of portfolio allows you to focus attention on specific functions, vocabulary items, and grammar points.

Collaborative Selection   A third option is some combination of the two approaches described above. You can assign specific activities from which students may choose what to include in their portfolios, or you can assign some specific activities and allow the students to choose others on their own. The collaborative approach allows you to focus on specific objectives, while at the same time giving students the opportunity to showcase what they feel is their best work.

As the classroom teacher, you are in the best position to decide what type of portfolio is most beneficial for your program and students. The most important step is to decide what objectives and outcomes the portfolio should assess, and then assign or help students select items that will best reflect those objectives and outcomes.

Chapter-Specific Portfolio Suggestions

Specific portfolio suggestions, one written and one oral, are provided for each chapter. These suggestions are based on existing *Pupil's Edition* activities that have been expanded to incorporate most of the functions and the vocabulary for each chapter. These materials may be included in the students' portfolios or used as guidelines for the inclusion of other materials.

Using the Portfolio Checklists

The checklists on pages 14 and 15 will help you and your students keep their portfolios organized. The *Student's Portfolio Checklist* is designed to help students track the items they include. The *Teacher's Portfolio Checklist* is a list of the items you expect students to include. If you choose to allow students to select materials for their portfolios, your checklist list will be very general, specifying only the types of items and the dates on which each item should be included. Your checklist will be more specific if you are assigning specific portfolio activities, as it should indicate the particular activities you have assigned and the dates on which they are to be included.

Peer Editing

Peer editing provides students an excellent opportunity to help each other develop writing skills. It also promotes an atmosphere of responsibility and teamwork through the writing process. We have included a *Peer Editing Rubric* to encourage peer editing in the classroom, and to aid students in this part of the evaluation process. Using the rubric, students can exchange compositions (usually a first draft), and edit each other's work according to a clearly designed, step-by-step process. The rubric is divided into three parts. Part I helps students examine the overall content of the written assignment using specific question prompts concerning vocabulary, organization, detail, and description. Part II helps students examine grammar and mechanics. In this part, you can tailor the goal of the assignment by outlining for the students the specific functions and grammar on which their editing should focus. For example, in Chapter 3, you might choose to focus on adjective agreement, or, in Chapter 5, you might choose functions for ordering food and beverages. Use the space labeled "Target

Functions and Grammar" in the *Peer Editing Rubric* for this purpose. Part III asks students to discuss the first two parts of the rubric in an effort to have them evaluate each other's work critically. Even though the rubric is organized in a step-by-step manner, your help in addressing students' questions will further increase the effectiveness of the peer editing process. The *Peer Editing Rubric* can be used with any written assignment.

Documenting Group Work

Very often a group-work project cannot be included in an individual's portfolio because of its size or the difficulties involved in making copies for each group member (posters, bulletin boards, videos, and so on). Other group or pair activities, such as conversations or skits, cannot be included in the portfolio unless they are recorded. To help students document such activities in their portfolios, you may want to use the *Documentation of Group Work* form on page 13.

Evaluating the Total Portfolio

Exactly how and how often you evaluate your students' complete portfolios will depend on the stated purpose. Ideally, students' portfolios should be evaluated at regular intervals over the course of the academic year. You should establish the length of the assessment period in advance—six weeks, a quarter, a semester, and so on. The *Portfolio Self-Evaluation* and *Portfolio Evaluation* forms on pages 16–17 are designed to aid you and your students in assessing the portfolio at the end of each assessment period. In order to ensure that portfolios are progressing successfully, you might want to meet individually with each student throughout each assessment period. In addition, individual conferences with students should be scheduled at the end of each evaluation period to discuss their portfolios and compare your assessment with their own. For further information about portfolio assessment, see pages T40–T41 of the *Annotated Teacher's Edition*.

Performance Assessment

Performance assessment provides an alternative to traditional testing methods by using authentic situations as contexts for performing communicative, competency-based tasks. For every chapter of the *Pupil's Edition,* this guide provides performance assessment suggestions to go with each **étape** of the chapter and one suggestion for global performance assessment that involves vocabulary and functions from the entire chapter. These suggestions give students the opportunity to demonstrate both acquired language proficiency and cultural competence in interviews, conversations, dialogues, or skits that can be performed for the entire class, or recorded or videotaped for evaluation at a later time. Performance assessment recordings can be included in student portfolios, or used independently, according to your needs for oral evaluation.

Using CD-ROM for Assessment

The *Allez, viens! Interactive CD-ROM Tutor* provides a unique tool for evaluating students' language proficiency and for incorporating technology in the classroom. CD-ROM technology appeals to a variety of student learning styles, and offers you an efficient means by which to gauge student progress. This guide provides instructions for written activities, such as lists, letters, e-mail, journal entries, and advertisements. Oral activities include conversations, interviews, and dialogues. Writing and recording features also enable you to create your own activities and to evaluate student work according to your particular needs. Student work can be saved to a disk and included in students' portfolios.

Rubrics and Evaluation Guidelines

Oral Rubric A

Use the following criteria to evaluate oral assignments. For assignments where comprehension is difficult to evaluate, you might want to give students full credit for comprehension or weigh other categories more heavily.

	4	**3**	**2**	**1**
Content	Complete	Generally complete	Somewhat complete	Incomplete
	Speaker consistently uses the appropriate functions and vocabulary necessary to communicate.	Speaker usually uses the appropriate functions and vocabulary necessary to communicate.	Speaker sometimes uses the appropriate functions and vocabulary necessary to communicate.	Speaker uses few of the appropriate functions and vocabulary necessary to communicate.
Comprehension	Total comprehension	General comprehension	Moderate comprehension	Little comprehension
	Speaker understands all of what is said to him or her.	Speaker understands most of what is said to him or her.	Speaker understands some of what is said to him or her.	Speaker understands little of what is said to him or her.
Comprehensibility	Comprehensible	Usually comprehensible	Sometimes comprehensible	Seldom comprehensible
	Listener understands all of what the speaker is trying to communicate.	Listener understands most of what the speaker is trying to communicate.	Listener understands less than half of what the speaker is trying to communicate.	Listener understands little of what the speaker is trying to communicate.
Accuracy	Accurate	Usually accurate	Sometimes accurate	Seldom accurate
	Speaker uses language correctly, including grammar, spelling, word order, and punctuation.	Speaker usually uses language correctly, including grammar, spelling, word order, and punctuation.	Speaker has some problems with language usage.	Speaker makes many errors in language usage.
Fluency	Fluent	Moderately fluent	Somewhat fluent	Not fluent
	Speaker speaks clearly without hesitation. Pronunciation and intonation sound natural.	Speaker has few problems with hesitation, pronunciation, and/or intonation.	Speaker has some problems with hesitation, pronunciation, and/or intonation.	Speaker hesitates frequently and struggles with pronunciation and intonation.

Oral Rubric B

Assignment _____

Targeted function(s) _____

_____

Targeted vocabulary _____

Targeted grammar _____

Content	You used the functions and vocabulary necessary to communicate.	(Excellent)	4	3	2	1	(Poor)	
Comprehension	You understood what was said to you and responded appropriately.	(Excellent)	4	3	2	1	(Poor)	
Comprehensibility	The listener was able to understand what you were trying to communicate.	(Excellent)	4	3	2	1	(Poor)	
Accuracy	You used language correctly, including grammar, spelling, word order, and punctuation.	(Excellent)	4	3	2	1	(Poor)	
Fluency	You spoke clearly and without hesitation. Your pronunciation and intonation sounded natural.	(Excellent)	4	3	2	1	(Poor)	

Total Score _____

Comments _____

_____

_____

French 1 Allez, viens!

Oral Progress Report

OVERALL IMPRESSION

☐ Excellent ☐ Good ☐ Satisfactory ☐ Unsatisfactory

Some particularly good aspects of this item are _____

_____

_____

_____

_____

Some areas that could be improved are _____

_____

_____

_____

_____

To improve your speaking, I recommend _____

_____

_____

_____

_____

Additional Comments _____

_____

_____

_____

_____

Written Rubric A

Use the following criteria to evaluate written assignments.

	4	**3**	**2**	**1**
Content	**Complete**	**Generally complete**	**Somewhat complete**	**Incomplete**
	Writer uses the appropriate functions and vocabulary for the topic.	Writer usually uses the appropriate functions and vocabulary for the topic.	Writer uses few of the appropriate functions and vocabulary for the topic.	Writer uses none of the appropriate functions and vocabulary for the topic.
Comprehensibility	**Comprehensible**	**Usually comprehensible**	**Sometimes comprehensible**	**Seldom comprehensible**
	Reader can understand all of what the writer is trying to communicate.	Reader can understand most of what the writer is trying to communicate.	Reader can understand less than half of what the writer is trying to communicate.	Reader can understand little of what the writer is trying to communicate.
Accuracy	**Accurate**	**Usually accurate**	**Sometimes accurate**	**Seldom accurate**
	Writer uses grammar, spelling, word order, and punctuation correctly.	Writer usually uses grammar, spelling, word order, and punctuation correctly.	Writer has some problems with language usage.	Writer makes a significant number of errors in language usage.
Organization	**Well-organized**	**Generally well-organized**	**Somewhat organized**	**Poorly organized**
	Presentation is logical and effective.	Presentation is generally logical and effective with a few minor problems.	Presentation is somewhat illogical and confusing in places.	Presentation lacks logical order and organization.
Effort	**Excellent effort**	**Good effort**	**Moderate effort**	**Minimal effort**
	Writer exceeds the requirements of the assignment and has put care and effort into the process.	Writer fulfills all of the requirements of the assignment.	Writer fulfills some of the requirements of the assignment.	Writer fulfills few of the requirements of the assignment.

French 1 Allez, viens!

Written Rubric B

Assignment _____

Targeted function(s) _____

_____

Targeted vocabulary _____

Targeted grammar _____

Content	You used the functions and vocabulary necessary to communicate.	(Excellent)	4	3	2	1	(Poor)
Organization	Your presentation was logical and effective.	(Excellent)	4	3	2	1	(Poor)
Comprehensibility	The reader was able to understand what you were trying to communicate.	(Excellent)	4	3	2	1	(Poor)
Accuracy	You used grammar, spelling, word order, and punctuation correctly.	(Excellent)	4	3	2	1	(Poor)
Effort	You put a lot of thought and effort into this assignment.	(Excellent)	4	3	2	1	(Poor)

Total Score _____

Comments _____

_____

_____

_____

Written Progress Report

OVERALL IMPRESSION

☐ Excellent ☐ Good ☐ Satisfactory ☐ Unsatisfactory

Some particularly good aspects of this item are _____

_____

_____

_____

_____

Some areas that could be improved are _____

_____

_____

_____

_____

To improve your written work, I recommend _____

_____

_____

_____

_____

_____

Additional Comments _____

_____

_____

_____

_____

_____

Peer Editing Rubric

Chapter _____

I. Content: Look for the following elements in your partner's composition. Put a check next to each category when you finish it.

1. _____ Vocabulary | Does the composition use enough new vocabulary from the chapter? Underline all the new vocabulary words you find from this chapter. What additional words do you suggest that your partner try to use?

2. _____ Organization | Is the composition organized and easy to follow? Can you find an introduction and a conclusion?

3. _____ Comprehensibility | Is the composition clear and easy to understand? Is there a specific part that was hard to understand? Did you understand the author's meaning? Draw a box around any sections that were particularly hard to understand.

4. _____ Target Functions and Grammar | Ask your teacher what functions and grammar you should focus on for this chapter and list them below.

Focus: _____

II. Proofreader's checklist: Circle any errors you find in your partner's composition, so that your partner can correct them. See the chart for some examples.

Incorrect form of the verb	*aime* J'(aimes) le cinéma.
Adjective – noun agreement Subject – verb agreement	*intelligentes* Mes amies sont (intelligents.) *vont* Elles (va) à la plage.
Spelling	*seize* Il a (sieze) ans.
Article	*la* Il aime (le) glace.
Transition words (if they apply to chapter)	d'abord, ensuite, après, enfin, etc...
Accents and Punctuation	*vélo* Je fais du (velo).

III. Explain your content and grammar suggestions to your partner. Answer any questions about your comments.

Peer editor's signature: _____ Date: _____

Portfolio Suggestions

Documentation of Group Work

Item _____ Chapter _____

Group Members: _____
_____
_____
_____

Description of Item: _____
_____
_____
_____
_____
_____
_____
_____
_____

Personal Contribution: _____
_____
_____
_____
_____
_____
_____
_____
_____
_____
_____

Please rate your personal contribution to the group's work.

☐ Excellent   ☐ Good   ☐ Satisfactory   ☐ Unsatisfactory

Student's Portfolio Checklist

To the Student   This form should be used to keep track of the materials you are including in your portfolio. It is important that you keep this list up-to-date so that your portfolio will be complete at the end of the assessment period. As you build your portfolio, try to include pieces of your work that show progress in your ability to speak and write French.

	Type of Item	Date Completed	Date Placed in Portfolio
Item #1			
Item #2			
Item #3			
Item #4			
Item #5			
Item #6			
Item #7			
Item #8			
Item #9			
Item #10			
Item #11			
Item #12			

Teacher's Portfolio Checklist

To the Teacher   This form should be used to keep track of the materials you expect your students to keep in their portfolios for the semester. Encourage students to keep their lists up-to-date so that their portfolios will be complete at the end of the assessment period.

	Type of Item	Date Assigned	Date Due in Portfolio
Item #1			
Item #2			
Item #3			
Item #4			
Item #5			
Item #6			
Item #7			
Item #8			
Item #9			
Item #10			
Item #11			
Item #12			

Portfolio Self-Evaluation

To the Student   Your portfolio consists of selections of your written and oral work. You should consider all the items in your portfolio as you evaluate your progress. Read the statements below and mark a box to the right of each statement to show how well you think your portfolio demonstrates your skills and abilities in French.

	Strongly Agree	Agree	Disagree	Strongly Disagree
1. My portfolio contains all the required items.				
2. My portfolio provides evidence of my progress in speaking and writing French.				
3. The items in my portfolio demonstrate that I can communicate my ideas in French.				
4. The items in my portfolio demonstrate accurate use of French.				
5. The items in my portfolio show that I understand and can use a wide variety of vocabulary.				
6. When I created the items in my portfolio, I tried to use what I had learned in new ways.				
7. The items in my portfolio provide an accurate picture of my skills and abilities in French.				

The item I like best in my portfolio is _____

because (please give at least three reasons) _____

_____

_____

_____

_____

_____

_____

_____

I find my portfolio to be (check one):

☐ Excellent   ☐ Good   ☐ Satisfactory   ☐ Unsatisfactory

Portfolio Evaluation

To the Student   I have reviewed the items in your portfolio and want to share with you my reactions to your work.

Teacher's Signature _____

Date _____

	Strongly Agree	Agree	Disagree	Strongly Disagree
1. Your portfolio contains all the required items.				
2. Your portfolio provides evidence of your progress in speaking and writing French.				
3. The items in your portfolio demonstrate that you can communicate your ideas in French.				
4. The items in your portfolio demonstrate accurate use of French.				
5. The items in your portfolio demonstrate the use of a wide variety of French vocabulary.				
6. The items in your portfolio demonstrate that you have tried to use what you have learned in new ways.				
7. The items in your portfolio provide an accurate picture of your skills and abilities in French.				

The item I like best in your portfolio is _____

because _____

_____

_____

One area in which you seem to need improvement is _____

_____

For your next portfolio collection, I would like to suggest _____

_____

I find your portfolio to be (check one):

☐ Excellent   ☐ Good   ☐ Satisfactory   ☐ Unsatisfactory

Faisons connaissance!

Portfolio Suggestions

Oral: Mise en pratique Activity 3

Expanded Activity Have students work in groups of three or four. Students should imagine they're going to meet a French-speaking exchange student and introduce the student to some of their American friends. First, have students write down the questions they'll need to ask in order to find out the exchange student's name, age, likes, and dislikes. Then they should act out the interview and introduction, with one student being the interviewer, the other, the exchange student. Students should change roles until everyone has had a chance to play both roles.

Purpose to practice asking for someone's name, age, likes, and dislikes; to ask and answer questions; to make introductions

Rationale Simulating real situations helps students use the language actively, thus accelerating their learning.

Materials audio or video recorder and player and individual cassettes

Portfolio Item Have students record the interview and introductions for inclusion in their portfolios.

Written: Mise en pratique Activity 5

Expanded Activity Have students continue the letter they wrote to Robert by telling him about a friend who would like to have a pen pal. Students should include information about the friend's age, likes, and dislikes.

Purpose to practice giving someone's name and age and describing their likes and dislikes

Rationale Applying the targeted functional expressions to a real-life situation reinforces students' retention of the material.

Materials pencil or pen and paper

Portfolio Item Students may want to include all drafts of the letter in their portfolios to show progress, or they may want to include only the final version.

Vive l'école!

Oral: Activity 22

Expanded Activity Have students pair off and exchange the class schedules they have prepared. After reading each other's schedules, partners should discuss them. They should find out whether their partner likes or dislikes certain classes and which classes they have together. Partners should share opinions about the classes they both have.

Purpose to practice asking for and giving information about classes; to give opinions; to give information; to agree and disagree; to tell time

Rationale Discussing schedules and courses is interesting and relevant to students' lives.

Materials audio or video recorder and player and individual cassettes

Portfolio Item Have students make an audio or video recording of their conversations for their portfolio.

Written: Activity 26

Expanded Activity Have students evaluate the school year so far, telling what they think of their courses, activities, and teachers. They should tell what part of the day they like best and what this year is like for them.

Purpose to practice new vocabulary and review previous grammar; to give information and express opinions; to write about classes; to agree and disagree

Rationale Using language skills in discussing real-life situations aids students' retention of the language.

Materials pencil or pen and paper

Portfolio Item Have students include their written evaluation in their portfolios.

Tout pour la rentrée

Written: Mise en pratique Activity 3

Expanded Activity Have students work with a partner to create their own catalogue of back-to-school merchandise. As a prewriting activity, have students look through catalogues to see what kind of information is included on an authentic catalogue page. Then have students write a description of each item in their catalogue, including an order number and price. Have students use the Peer Editing Rubric on *Alternative Assessment Guide* page 9 to check each other's work for spelling and grammar. Finally, have students draw illustrations or cut out pictures from catalogues and lay out the pages.

Purpose to reinforce vocabulary learned; to describe merchandise found in a store; to make and respond to requests

Rationale Creating visual images of their descriptions reinforces the meaning of the language, fosters accuracy, and appeals to visual learners.

Materials large paper; colored and black felt pens; scissors; catalogues or magazines for pictures; pencil or pen

Portfolio Items The catalogue pages and all drafts of the description could be included in each student's portfolio.

Oral: Mise en pratique Activity 4

This oral activity is a continuation of the written one above.

Expanded Activity Have students exchange the catalogue pages they created in the written portfolio activity with those of another group. Using the new catalogue pages, students should take turns with their partner ordering items "over the phone." When phoning, students should remember to greet the person taking the order, using appropriate titles and **vous,** and ask about the merchandise. The customer and the person taking the order over the telephone should sit back-to-back to simulate a telephone conversation where speakers cannot see each other.

Purpose to practice talking on the phone; to express need and ask others what they need; to ask for and give information

Rationale Telephoning in a foreign language is difficult since the speakers cannot see each other's facial expressions or body language. This is an excellent opportunity to sharpen listening skills, to ask for repetition and clarification, and to be sure pronunciation is accurate enough to convey meaning.

Materials catalogue pages created in the written portfolio activity; two telephones; audio recorder; individual cassettes

Portfolio Item The audio recording of the telephone conversation should be incorporated into the portfolio.

Sports et passe-temps

Portfolio Suggestions

Oral: Activity 24

Expanded Activity Have students work in pairs to plan an imaginary vacation together. First, students should make suggestions and decide on a season and a month to take their vacation. Then have them take account of the different types of weather typical for the season they choose and tell which activities they like to do in the different weather conditions. Finally, students should decide on some activities they both like to do and make an all-weather plan for their vacation together. Have students record their conversation on audiocassette or videocassette.

Purpose to practice vocabulary for weather, seasons, and months, as well as hobbies, and pastimes; to practice making plans with another person

Rationale Language skills should be practiced in realistic situations. Making plans with another person requires students to use the language in a context that simulates a real-life speaking situation.

Materials audio or video recorder and player; individual cassettes

Portfolio Item Each student could record all the steps of the activity and include the complete recording in his or her portfolio.

Written: Activity 31

Expanded Activity Based on the information students gathered from their classmates in Part b of Activity 31, have them invent a description for an ideal summer camp (**colonie de vacances**). First students should list the activities their classmates like to do during the summer. Then they should choose a location and write a description of what the weather is like, what sports and activities teenagers do at the camp, and how often they do them. (**On fait souvent de la natation.**)

Purpose to practice new vocabulary for sports, places, and weather; to use adverbs of frequency

Rationale Giving students the opportunity to write about things that have personal meaning will motivate them to communicate in the foreign language.

Materials pencil or pen and paper

Portfolio Item Each step of the writing activity could be included in students' portfolios, parts a and b of Activity 31 as well as the final description of a summer camp.

5 On va au café?

Oral: Mise en pratique Activity 2

Expanded Activity Have students work in groups of three or four to create posters and signs for one of the three cafés shown on page 164 of the textbook. The signs should include a menu, prices, specials, advertisements for various beverages (mineral water, soda, coffee, tea, and so on). Using these signs, students should create a set for a café in which to perform a skit. They might decorate three areas in the classroom to represent the three cafés. Students in each group decide who the server is; the others are the customers. The members of each group visit one of the two cafés they did not create. Before visiting a café, each group should write a conversation in which they enter a café, ask the waiter questions about the selections, decide what to order from the menu, place their order, receive their food, comment on the food, ask for the check, pay, thank the waiter, and leave the restaurant. Students should practice the conversation orally in their groups before performing their skit. You may want to record their performances on audio- or videocassette.

Purpose to practice vocabulary about restaurants and food; to get someone's attention; to order food; to make suggestions; to inquire; to express likes and dislikes; to pay the check; to create a café menu; to order from a menu

Rationale The vocabulary associated with ordering food in a café or restaurant is very specific and should be practiced so that students feel confident in dealing with this important aspect of French life.

Materials newsprint or posterboard; tape; colored and black felt-tipped pens; audio or video recorder and player; individual cassettes

Portfolio Item Each student should include the audio or video recording of the conversation in the café in his or her portfolio.

Written: Activity 24

Expanded Activity Have students write a longer letter to a new pen pal. Students should tell their name and age, their favorite and least favorite classes, their favorite and least favorite after-school activities, and what they eat and drink when they go out with their friends.

Purpose to combine previously learned material; to tell your name and age; to describe school subjects; to tell about after-school activities; to describe food and beverages

Rationale Writing a letter will allow students to combine and review many of the functions learned up to this point.

Materials pencil or pen and paper

Portfolio Item Students may want to include all drafts of the letter in their portfolio to show progress, or they may choose to include only the final version.

Oral: Activity 27

Expanded Activity Have students look at a large map of Paris that includes the location of landmarks and tourist attractions. The class should suggest places to go in the city. The places can include tourist attractions or ordinary locations such as a movie theater. List on the board all the places students suggest. Divide the class into groups. Each group member writes the name of a place, the day he or she is going there, and the time on a slip of paper (**la tour Eiffel, dimanche, 14h00**). The group members first ask yes-no questions to try to find out where one person is going (**Tu vas à Notre-Dame?**). When group members guess where their classmate is going, they need to find out exactly when (**Tu y vas samedi? Tu y vas à 13h00?**). When all the information is known, the student invites each group member individually to go along (**Tu viens?**). The group members accept or refuse. When every group member has had a turn to invite the others, they should all make plans for the weekend, deciding where to go, when to go, and where they will meet.

Purpose to make plans; to extend invitations; to arrange to meet someone; to talk about time; to practice asking information questions

Rationale Repetition of questions helps students internalize the forms. Group work maximizes practice time, develops social skills, and fosters cooperative learning.

Materials audio or video equipment and individual cassettes

Portfolio Item Make an audio or video recording of each group's final conversation for their portfolios.

Written: Activity 31

Expanded Activity Based on the decisions made by the groups in the oral activity above, students write a journal entry telling where they and their friends are going to go in Paris this weekend. They should include where they are going, what time they are going there, and where they will meet.

Purpose to reinforce comprehension by writing what was spoken; to rely on listening skills to recall what was said in French and to report it in French

Rationale Making plans and setting times is a valuable skill in any language.

Materials pencil or pen and paper

Portfolio Item The written journal entries should be included in individual portfolios.

PORTFOLIO SUGGESTIONS

Oral: Activity 25

Expanded Activity Have students work in groups. One student has a friend staying over for the weekend. As they are doing chores on Saturday, various family members come and go. Students should introduce each family member to their friend and tell a little bit about them (name, age, character description, and so on). Group members should take turns so that everyone has a chance to describe his or her family members.

Purpose to introduce and describe people; to practice giving names and ages; to practice using possessive adjectives

Rationale Talking about real-life situations motivates students to communicate in the new language.

Materials personal photographs or pictures from magazines to represent real or imaginary family members; audio or video recorder and player; individual cassettes

Portfolio Item Each group could record its session on audiocassette or videocassette and have copies made to include in each student's portfolio. Students could also include any notes created during the activity.

Written: Activity 25

This activity is a continuation of the oral one above.

Expanded Activity Members of each group should exchange real or imaginary family pictures. Using any notes they may have taken during the oral session, students should write about their partner's pictures. They should give names, ages, relationships, and describe personalities, interests, and hobbies. Students should also paste pictures and descriptions together to form photo album pages, which could be combined with other students' pages to form a class album.

Purpose to introduce and describe people; to practice giving names and ages; to practice using possessive adjectives

Rationale Students need practice writing about subjects that are relevant to their lives. They will develop the ability to describe people and things.

Materials pencil or pen and paper; photocopies of the pictures

Portfolio Items The descriptions of the partner's pictures, as well as the photo album page, could be included in the students' portfolio.

Written: Activity 26

Expanded Activity Have students create a script for a television commercial to promote a food they like to eat. The commercial could be as simple as a jingle to accompany pictures and logos they create or as involved as a paragraph promoting the advantages of the product. Have students brainstorm to come up with ideas for the commercial, create a rough draft, and write a final script.

Purpose to use the functions and vocabulary from this chapter in a creative and entertaining way

Rationale Imaginative, creative use of the language that goes beyond the everyday use of French develops creative writing skills, appeals to different learning styles, and is enjoyable and motivating.

Materials newsprint, posterboard, and colored paper; colored pens; magazine pictures of the food item selected; pencil or pen and paper

Portfolio Items Copies of the brainstorming notes, the rough draft, and the final draft of the commercial could be included in each student's portfolio to show the complete writing process.

Oral: Activity 28

This oral activity is a continuation of the written one above.

Expanded Activity Using the advertisement created in the written portfolio item, students act out a follow-up interview between a nutrition expert and the manufacturer of the product, who is trying to promote sales of the product. The nutrition expert should be asked to describe the food group(s) the product represents (see chart on page 256 of the textbook), the nutritional benefit of the product, how often one should consume it, and so on. Students should write and revise the script before performing it.

Purpose to practice functional expressions learned in this chapter within a different context; to ask for information in an interview setting; to respond to questions

Rationale Students are able to practice question formation and manipulate a broad range of language and vocabulary in creative activities such as a TV interview.

Materials advertisements created in the written portfolio activity; pencil or pen and paper; audio or video recorder and player; individual cassettes

Portfolio Items Each student should include a copy of the script as well as an audio or video recording of the interview in his or her portfolio.

CHAPITRE
9

Au téléphone

Written: Activity 17
Oral: Activity 28

Expanded Activity *(In this chapter, oral and written portfolio suggestions are combined.)*
Students should work in pairs. One partner writes a list of the six worst things that happened to him or her during the past week—real or imagined. The other partner writes about six wonderful things—real or imagined—that happened to him or her during the past week. They describe the circumstances in detail, such as where they went, who was with them, and so on. Then, while one partner describes his or her week, the other asks questions to clarify details and takes notes to help him or her remember what happened. Have partners exchange roles and repeat the exercise. Record each of the conversations. Finally, each student writes a report on his or her partner's activities during the past week.

Purpose to practice the past tense; to ask for and express opinions; to inquire about and relate past events; to clarify details; to share confidences; to console and congratulate others

Rationale Students need to be able to recount new and unexpected events, tell and write their stories clearly, ask for clarification, make appropriate responses, and remember and express details in the new language.

Materials pencil or pen and paper; audio or video recorder and player; individual cassettes

Portfolio Items Students should include a copy of the written report in their portfolios, along with a copy of the audiocassette or videocassette.

Dans un magasin de vêtements

Portfolio Suggestions

Written: Activity 16

Expanded Activity Ask your students to write a report on what people are wearing in school. Have them identify different clothing styles prevalent among the students. Students should describe the style, color, and fit of the clothes in their report and give their opinions of the different styles. Based on their findings, have students create a page of a fashion catalogue, including prices and descriptions of each item.

Purpose to describe clothes, using appropriate vocabulary; to give an opinion

Rationale Students should practice observing and describing their surroundings in the new language.

Materials pencil or pen and paper

Portfolio Items The written report on clothing worn in school and the fashion catalogue page could be included in the students' portfolios.

Oral: Activity 33

Expanded Activity Students should bring fashion magazines and catalogues to class. Have students look through them to find two outfits—one they really like and one they dislike. Create small conversation groups. Discussion in each group should focus on the color, style, fit, and cost of the clothes. Encourage group members to share their opinions freely, agreeing or disagreeing with their classmates' assessment of the outfits.

Purpose to ask for and give advice; to ask for an opinion; to pay a compliment; to criticize, hesitate, and make a decision

Rationale Clothing and fashion are important to most teenagers. Students should be able to discuss this subject in the new language.

Materials fashion magazines and catalogues (the school library is a possible source of these); audio or video recorder and player; individual cassettes

Portfolio Item An audio or video recording of the group conversation should be included in the students' portfolios.

 **Vive les vacances!**

CHAPITRE

Written: Activity 28

Expanded Activity Have students expand their notes into letters by asking about the weather where their friend is going as well as what there is to see and do there. Then have students exchange letters and answer them as if they were the friend who is on vacation. You might suggest that students use the information they've learned about the weather, tourist sites, leisure time activities, and sports.

Purpose to incorporate cultural material into the writing process; to ask questions and respond appropriately; to write a letter

Rationale Writing from a different cultural perspective encourages students to focus on the cultural information they've learned.

Materials pencil or pen and paper

Portfolio Item The written questions and the final version of the letter should be included in the portfolio.

Oral: Activity 32

Expanded Activity Each student should make a poster about his or her last vacation or an imaginary vacation. The poster might include personal photos, pictures from a travel brochure, drawings, and so on. Each picture should have a caption describing it. Display the completed posters around the classroom. Working with a partner, students ask questions about their partner's poster—what the place was like, who was there, what the activities were, what he or she liked best and least about the vacation, whether or not he or she is planning to return in the future, and why. Before starting the activity, you might have the class brainstorm to create a list of possible questions. Write these on the board for students to use in creating a questionnaire, which they can fill out as they interview their partner.

Purpose to inquire about and share past events and future plans; to ask for and express opinions; to describe vacation spots and vacation activities; to reinforce new vocabulary; to practice listening, taking notes, and asking for clarification

Rationale Students will retain new language skills better when they talk about real-life situations. Vacation vocabulary is important for potential future travelers to francophone countries.

Materials posterboard; photographs; illustrated travel magazines and brochures; colored markers, glue, pushpins, pens; audio or video recorder and player; individual cassettes

Portfolio Item An audio or video recording of the interview should be incorporated into the oral portfolio. Students could also include their posters.

En ville

Oral: Activity 13

Expanded Activity

Have students use the map they have created. They should make sure that at least five buildings and all streets are labeled. Then students should create a copy of this map, deleting the names of the buildings, but keeping the street names. Partners should exchange the unlabeled maps.

Each student should create cards on which he or she records an errand that can be done at each location on the map—one errand per card. The game starts at the school. Students take turns drawing from their partner's pile of cards. One student reads aloud the errand on the card. His or her partner gives directions to the appropriate destination without naming the place, starting from the school if they're just beginning, or from the student's last position on the map. Students gain points for successfully following directions, and lose points for not following directions or giving wrong directions.

Purpose to practice asking for and giving directions; to identify places; to write about directions and events using sequencing words

Rationale Students need to know how to ask for and give directions if they are in a French-speaking country or to help a French-speaking visitor.

Materials copies of map; pencils, erasers, markers; index cards; scissors; audio or video recorder and player; individual cassettes

Portfolio Item An audio or video recording of the game should be included in the students' portfolios.

Written: Activity 30

Expanded Activity Have students work with a partner. Students should write questions to ask about their partner's neighborhood. Based on their partner's answers, students should draw a map of their partner's neighborhood.

Purpose to ask questions and respond appropriately; to reinforce vocabulary learned in the chapter; to practice using prepositions

Rationale Being able to give directions and convey information in a clear manner is important in any language.

Materials pencil or pen and paper

Portfolio Item The questions and the map of the partner's neighborhood should be incorporated into each student's portfolio.

Performance
Assessment

Faisons connaissance!

Première étape

Have students act out their conversations from Activity 16, page 25 of the *Pupil's Edition,* using the appropriate gestures.

Deuxième étape

Have students make a collage of the things they like and dislike. See page 15C of the *Annotated Teacher's Edition* for a full description of this project. You might refer students to the Additional Vocabulary, which begins on page R9 of the *Pupil's Edition,* for additional likes and dislikes. Have students present their collages to the class, telling whether they like or dislike each of the objects pictured.

Troisième étape

When students have finished Activity 28 on page 34 of the *Pupil's Edition,* have them pair off and take turns interviewing the celebrities they have chosen. The interviewer might use a dummy microphone, and the celebrity might dress in an identifiable costume. If possible, have students videotape their interviews.

Global Performance Assessment

Have students imagine that a French exchange student has just arrived at your school. Ask them to work with a partner to brainstorm how they could find out the exchange student's name, age, likes, and dislikes. Then have each pair act out the the scene, taking turns playing the role of the French student.

Vive l'école!

Première étape

Have partners prepare and act out a conversation between a student and a school counselor in which they discuss the student's interests and the subjects he or she likes and dislikes.

Deuxième étape

Have students write their schedules entirely in French, including days, classes, and times according to the 24-hour clock. Then have students pair off, ask each other what classes they have and when, and tell which subjects they like and dislike.

Troisième étape

Have students work in pairs to create a conversation between a French student and an American student, comparing and contrasting their school schedules and times. They should express opinions and agreement or disagreement.

Global Performance Assessment

Have students work in groups of three to talk about . . .

a. the subjects they like best and their opinions of them.

b. the subjects they don't like and their opinions of them.

c. whether or not they agree with each other's likes and dislikes.

Tout pour la rentrée

Première étape

Show *Teaching Transparency 3-1.* Have students assume the identity of the shoppers and tell what they need for school.

Deuxième étape

Have students form groups, gather ten of their own school supplies, and make a list of the objects. Have one student tell what the group has. **(Nous avons ces stylos verts, cette calculatrice blanche...)**

Troisième étape

Have partners make lists of what they have and what they need for their courses. Then have them act out a scene in a store where they purchase the items they need.

Global Performance Assessment

Have students work in pairs. Each partner visits the "store" his or her partner created in Activity 7, page 99 of the *Pupil's Edition.* One partner plays the role of the salesperson, while the other gets the salesperson's attention, tells what he or she wants, asks for prices, pays for the purchases, thanks the salesperson, and says goodbye. The salesperson should respond appropriately. Then have students change roles. Remind the students to use **madame, monsieur,** or **mademoiselle,** and **vous.**

Sports et passe-temps

Première étape

Have pairs of students interview each other to find out their favorite and least favorite activities. You might have them act out their interviews for the class.

Deuxième étape

Have pairs of students create a conversation in which they talk about and compare what they like to do in each season of the year. Be sure that both students tell what they like to do and react to their partner's comments.

Troisième étape

Meet with students individually and have them respond orally to some of the questions in Activity 34, page 125 of the *Pupil's Edition.*

Global Performance Assessment

Have students work in pairs. One student plays the role of a famous Canadian athlete, the other plays a reporter for a local television station. The reporter interviews the athlete about his or her busy training routine. The athlete should tell what he or she does at different times of the year, in various weather conditions, and how often. Then have students change roles. The student playing the Canadian athlete should create a new identity and training routine.

On va au café?

Première étape

On a table, display food or beverage items or pictures of these items. Have students come up to the table. One asks for an item without pointing to it, saying **Je voudrais...** The other student picks up the correct item and hands it to his or her classmate, saying **Voilà.** Have students take turns asking for items.

Deuxième étape

Have students form groups of three: two customers and one server. They should enact a scene in a café in which the customers call the server, ask for the menu, ask the server some questions about the food, and order. The server responds accordingly.

Troisième étape

Have students form groups of three and act out a restaurant scene in which the customers order food, give opinions about it, and pay the check. The server should take and verify their orders and bring their check.

Global Performance Assessment

It's the day of the French Club annual picnic. Have students form small groups. Have one student act as host, the others as guests. The host asks people what they want. The guests will tell what they want and talk about how they like the food and drink. After eating, students suggest activities and decide which one they would like to participate in.

Amusons-nous!

Première étape

Have students write a letter to a French pen pal who is coming for a visit. Have them suggest what they can do during the pen pal's stay, using **on.**

Deuxième étape

Have students act out their dialogues from Activity 21, page 181 of the *Pupil's Edition.*

Troisième étape

Tell students that you'd like to join them for the activities they wrote about for Activity 31 on page 186 of the *Pupil's Edition.* Have them tell you what they are doing and when and where to meet. Alternatively, you might have students ask you about your weekend plans.

Global Performance Assessment

Divide the class into groups. Have students choose one place in Paris they'd all like to visit and decide on a meeting time and place. They should make sure that the Paris attraction they choose to visit will be open when they plan to go there. Have each group act out their conversation for the other students.

La famille

Première étape

Have students form groups of three. In each group, one person will introduce another to the third member. This person asks questions to get to know the newcomer, who can take on any identity. Have students present these introductions to the class.

Deuxième étape

Have students bring in a photo of someone and describe that person to the class, giving a physical description and telling what the person is like. The photo might be of a family member, a relative, a friend, or a famous person. Students might also choose to bring in a picture from a magazine.

Troisième étape

Have students write three things they would like to do and three chores they must do. Then tell them to pair off and create a skit in which a student asks a parent for permission to do something and the parent grants or refuses permission. Alternatively, students might create an oral or written monologue in which they complain about all the chores they have to do.

Global Performance Assessment

Have students work in groups to create a conversation for the following situation: Some teenagers arrive at a friend's front door, suggesting a place to go out. The teenager must ask for permission to go from his or her parent. The parent gives permission as long as the teenager finishes his or her chores first. The friends offer to help. As they work around the house, the teenagers discuss where to go and what to do. Tell students that they should be prepared to act out the scene using props.

Au marché

Première étape

Have students make a shopping list of at least five items, using the partitive articles. Then have them pair off and take turns asking what their partner needs.

Deuxième étape

In groups of four, students will plan a typical American dinner for a guest from Côte d'Ivoire. Have them make a grocery list **(Nous avons besoin de...)**. Then one student asks the others to go get the various items at the supermarket. The others respond appropriately.

Troisième étape

On separate index cards, write the names of the meals in French. Have students pair off and have one partner in each pair draw a card. Partners must then offer and accept or refuse four items that would normally be served at that meal. Encourage students to bring in food items, paper plates, and plastic eating utensils to make their skits more realistic.

Global Performance Assessment

First ask students to make a list in French of what they've eaten for the last two days. They should use food vocabulary they've learned in the chapter. Then have students pair off to role-play. One student seeks advice from the other, a nutrition counselor, about his or her diet based on the food list. The counselor tells what his or her partner should eat more of and what foods he or she shouldn't eat at all. The students should act out this scene, then change roles.

Au téléphone

Première étape

Have students imagine they are spending a weekend in Provence. Have them write a post-card home, telling what they did or didn't do. For a list of possible activities, refer students to the word box in Activity 12 on page 272 of the *Pupil's Edition.*

Deuxième étape

Have students act out a phone conversation between two friends who are asking about each other's weekends.

Troisième étape

Have students work in pairs to write a phone conversation in which one person brings up a problem and the other offers consolation and advice. Have students act it out in front of the class. If last year's class videotaped their skits, you might show them to get students started on their own conversations.

Global Performance Assessment

Have students work in pairs to create and act out a phone conversation in which one person is calling someone he or she hasn't spoken to in a while. One student should call a friend and ask to speak to him or her. The students should talk about what each of them did last weekend and find out what the other is planning to do next summer.

Dans un magasin de vêtements

Première étape

Have partners write and act out a short conversation between friends who are deciding what to wear to a school party that will include a picnic and dancing.

Deuxième étape

Have students perform their skits from Activity 25 on page 304 of the *Pupil's Edition,* with props. The skits may also be done by groups of three.

Troisième étape

Have students bring in a picture of an outfit from a magazine. Have them work in groups of three, with one person acting as the salesperson and the other two as friends. The friends ask for and give their opinions of each other's outfits and compliment or criticize the outfits. The salesperson offers help and compliments. Have students take turns playing the role of the salesperson.

Global Performance Assessment

Have students role-play a customer and a salesperson. The customer should choose one of the items from the advertisement on page 318 of the *Pupil's Edition.* Then the customer should ask the salesperson about it, finding out if the correct size is available, and if he or she can try it on. The salesperson should compliment the way it looks and the customer should decide whether to buy it or not. Students should take turns playing the role of salesperson.

Vive les vacances!

Première étape

Have students create radio commercials to promote their favorite vacation destination. They should describe the activities available there as well as the weather.

Deuxième étape

Have students write a note to a friend who is going on vacation. They should make up a destination, make suggestions about what to take and do, and say goodbye.

Troisième étape

Have students act out a phone conversation between two friends who are comparing their weekends. Students should tell how their weekends were and what they did.

Global Performance Assessment

Have students work in pairs to prepare the following scenes:

a. You want to take a trip for your vacation, but you're not sure where. Tell your travel agent what you like to do and what you'd like to see. The travel agent will make some suggestions about where you might go and what there is to do there. Ask about weather conditions and what clothes to take, where you can stay, and when and from where you can leave. The travel agent will answer appropriately and remind you of things you shouldn't forget to take.

b. You've returned from your trip and your friend wants to know how it went. Tell your friend about your trip and answer any questions he or she has about what you did.

Students should act out the scenes with a partner and then change roles.

En ville

Première étape

Have students write a note to a friend, telling all the things they plan to do over the weekend. They should include at least three chores, errands, or activities.

Deuxième étape

Write on index cards the names of items available at the places shown on page 359 of the *Pupil's Edition* **(du pain, de l'argent)**. Have students draw a card and ask a classmate to go to the appropriate place for it. **(Tu pourrais passer à la boulangerie?)** The partner responds accordingly. **(Je veux bien.)**

Troisième étape

Distribute maps or a section of a map of your city. Have students tell a partner how to get from the school to their house or another place in the city. The partner should follow along on the map and tell where the directions lead. Have students reverse roles. As an alternative, show *Teaching Transparency 12-3* and have students give directions to a place in Fort-de-France.

Global Performance Assessment

Have students work in pairs to create a scene between a post office employee and a tourist visiting Fort-de-France. The tourist should mail some postcards and ask for directions to two places in town: the library and the cathedral. Using the map on page 372 of the *Pupil's Edition,* the employee should give directions from the post office to each of the places. The tourist should ask questions if something is not clear. Then the tourist should ask what means of transportation he or she should use.

Using CD-ROM
for Assessment

Faisons connaissance!

Guided Recording

A toi de parler
Students record a conversation by responding to the following video prompts:
1. Salut.
2. Je m'appelle Mireille. Et toi? Tu t'appelles comment?
3. Comment ça va?
4. Tu as quel âge?
5. J'aime danser et parler au téléphone. Et toi? Qu'est-ce que tu aimes faire?

Guided Writing

A toi d'écrire
Students choose from among the following four writing scenarios:

 List A friend of yours who doesn't speak French is going to France on vacation. Create a list for his or her wallet that includes two ways to greet someone and three ways to say goodbye.

 List A French exchange student is going to your school and you and your friend want to get to know him or her better. List two or three things each of you likes to do, one thing neither of you likes to do, and two or three things you both like to do.

 E-mail You're contacting a girl from France on an Internet pen pal network. Write her an e-mail message telling your name and age and asking her age and some of her likes and dislikes.

 Journal Imagine you're going to be an exchange student in France. In your journal, write five questions you would use to get to know your new classmates.

Guided Recording

A toi de parler

Students record an interview by responding to the following video prompts:

1. Tu as quels cours le matin?
2. Tu as quoi l'après-midi?
3. Tu as français à quelle heure?
4. Comment tu trouves le cours de français?
5. Et le cours d'anglais, comment tu trouves ça?

Guided Writing

A toi d'écrire

Students choose from among the following four writing scenarios:

 Journal   Write a short paragraph about some of your classes. Mention two classes you like and two classes you dislike and tell why you like or don't like each of them.

 Script   Pauline and Marc are students in a French lycée. Pauline is planning to be a doctor and Marc wants to become a writer. Write a short dialogue in which the two of them discuss the classes they have and how they feel about them. They should tell which classes they like and dislike and why.

 Schedule   Create your ideal schedule. Include all of the classes you would like to have and the days and times you might have them.

 Survey   Imagine you're going to survey French students about their class schedules. Write five questions that you might ask. Then, have a partner respond to your questions as if he or she were a French student.

CD-ROM ASSESSMENT

Tout pour la rentrée

Guided Recording

A toi de parler

Students record a conversation based on the following prompts:

CUSTOMER	Get the salesperson's attention and ask for a backpack.
SALESPERSON	Tell the customer that you do have backpacks. Ask if he or she prefers black backpacks or green backpacks.
CUSTOMER	Ask the salesperson if he or she has any blue backpacks.
SALESPERSON	Tell the customer that you don't have any blue backpacks.
CUSTOMER	Tell the salesperson that you would like a blue backpack. Thank the salesperson.
SALESPERSON	Respond appropriately to the customer.

Guided Writing

A toi d'écrire

Students choose from among the following four writing scenarios:

 List Martin, a new French exchange student, has just arrived at your school and he has the same class schedule as you do. Create a list of supplies he will need for each class and mention anything else he might need. Begin your list with "Pour le français, il te faut..."

 Note Your locker is jammed, and you can't get any of your books or supplies. Write a note to a classmate asking to borrow the supplies you'll need for the next two class periods.

 List You've lost your backpack. Make a list of its contents so it can be identified. Be sure to include the color of each item.

 Survey Create a survey to find out what your classmates are buying this school year. Make a list of six to eight questions to ask your friends about their preferences in clothing, colors, and school supplies.

CD-ROM ASSESSMENT

Sports et passe-temps

 CD-ROM Assessment

Guided Recording

A toi de parler
Students record a conversation with a partner based on the following prompts:

STUDENT A Tell your partner two things you like to do. Then ask what your partner does for fun.

STUDENT B Tell your partner two things you like to do and one thing you really like to do. Ask if your partner likes to do the activity you really like.

STUDENT A Respond by saying how often you do the activity.

STUDENT B Invite your partner to do something he or she likes to do.

STUDENT A Accept or reject your partner's invitation.

Guided Writing

A toi d'écrire
Students choose from among the following four writing scenarios:

 Note Write a note to the French-Canadian exchange student who is coming to stay with you next year. He or she will arrive in September and wants to know what the weather is like and what there is to do in each season.

 List List the activities (real or imaginary) that you plan to do each day for the next two weeks. You may choose to put your list in the form of a calendar.

 Survey Create a six-to-eight-question survey to ask your classmates about sports and activities. Your survey should ask classmates to rate how much they like or dislike each activity and to tell how often they do each.

 Script Create a script in which two French-Canadian students are trying to decide what to do together on a cold winter weekend. One of the characters really likes sports and the other one prefers nonathletic activities.

On va au café?

Guided Recording

A toi de parler

Students record a conversation with a partner based on the following prompts:

SERVER	Greet the customer and ask if he or she has decided what to order.
CUSTOMER	Ask how much a food item from the menu costs.
SERVER	Give the price of the item.
CUSTOMER	Ask what drinks the restaurant serves.
SERVER	List the drinks that you have.
CUSTOMER	Order something to eat and drink.

Guided Writing

A toi d'écrire

Students choose among the following four writing scenarios:

 Note   Your friend wants to play soccer after school, but you're going to be busy. Write your friend a note and explain why you can't make it.

 Advertisement   Create a radio advertisement to promote a French café. In your ad, give the name of the café, tell what items you can eat and drink there, and describe how the food tastes.

 Menu   The French club is creating a sidewalk café for the International Fair at school. Create a menu for your café. Be sure to include the name of the café, the food and drink items available, and the prices.

 Script   Write a script for a comedy skit in which a customer is placing an order in a café. The customer can't decide what to order, and the server becomes frustrated.

CD-ROM Assessment

Guided Recording

A toi de parler
Students record a conversation with a partner based on the following prompts:

STUDENT A   Ask what your partner is going to do this weekend.

STUDENT B   Say that you don't have any special plans and ask what your partner is going to do.

STUDENT A   Tell one thing you're planning to do this weekend, and invite your partner to accompany you.

STUDENT B   Accept the invitation and ask when you should plan to meet.

STUDENT A   Tell when and where you will meet your partner.

STUDENT B   Indicate that you understand when and where to meet and say goodbye.

Guided Writing

A toi d'écrire
Students choose from among the following four writing scenarios.

 E-mail   Write an e-mail message in which you invite a friend to do something. Suggest three or four different activities and propose a meeting time and place.

 Survey   Create a survey to find out the most popular places in your area for teenagers to go. Ask six to eight questions about where teenagers like to go, when they go there, and with whom.

 Brochure   Create a brochure to encourage tourists to visit your town. Use the Process Writing steps below to complete your brochure.

 Note   Write a note inviting a friend to do something. Tell your friend about the activity you have planned, and tell when and where you'll meet. Also tell your friend if anyone else will be coming along.

PROCESS WRITING steps for **Brochure** assignment

PREWRITING Brainstorm some places of interest near your home and write a short list of activities you can do at each location.

WRITING Select four of the places from your PREWRITING list and write a 2-to-3 sentence paragraph encouraging your readers to visit each place. You may wish to leave space for illustrations.

REVISING Print out your brochure, make any necessary changes to improve it, and check it for correct spelling, accents, and capitalization.

PUBLISHING Correct any errors, rewrite anything you need to for greater clarity or emphasis and print out a copy of your finished brochure. You may wish to add illustrations to your brochure.

CD-ROM ASSESSMENT

La famille

Guided Recording

A toi de parler

Students record a conversation with a partner based on the following prompts:

CHILD	Ask your parent for permission to do something this weekend.
PARENT	Tell your child that he or she must do a certain chore first.
CHILD	Ask your parent if you can do the chore tomorrow.
PARENT	Grant permission.
CHILD	Thank your parent and tell him or her a time when you will do the chore.

Guided Writing

A toi d'écrire

Students choose from among the following four writing scenarios:

 Lost-and-Found Ad You've lost your pet (real or imaginary). Write a detailed description of your pet for the newspaper.

 Interview Imagine that you're interviewing the new French exchange student about his family and home life for your school newspaper. Write down five or six questions you'll ask and the exchange student's answers.

 Cast of Characters You're going to write a short story for a contest. Start off by writing detailed descriptions of at least two of the main characters.

 List of Chores You have to study for a big exam, so you can't do any of your chores this weekend. A friend has agreed to do your chores for you. Make a list of at least five chores your friend should do.

Guided Recording

A toi de parler

Students record a conversation with a partner based on the following prompts:

HOST/HOSTESS   Ask your guest if he or she would like some water.

GUEST   Accept or refuse the offer.

HOST/HOSTESS   Ask if your guest would like some more cake.

GUEST   Accept the offer.

HOST/HOSTESS   Ask if your guest likes the cake.

GUEST   Express an opinion about the cake.

Guided Writing

A toi d'écrire

Students choose from among the following four writing scenarios:

 List   You're going on an overnight camping trip with two friends and you're in charge of planning the meals. List the foods you'll need, the quantity of each item, and tell at what meal you plan to eat each item.

 Conversation   Create an 8-to-10-line conversation between two people who are eating a meal together. Be sure to include offering and accepting or refusing food in the conversation.

 Newspaper article   You're a travel reporter writing an article about a market in Côte d'Ivoire. Write about the foods available at the market. Be sure to mention any foods that might be unfamiliar to your readers.

 Menu   You're a nutritionist. Create menus for two days of healthful meals for a new client. Be sure to include a variety of foods from all of the food groups.

CD-ROM ASSESSMENT

Au téléphone

Guided Recording

A toi de parler

Students record a phone conversation by responding to the following video prompts:

1. Allô?
2. Qui est à l'appareil?
3. Une seconde. Ne quitte pas... Désolé(e)! Elle n'est pas là.
4. D'accord.
5. Bien sûr. Au revoir.

Guided Writing

A toi d'écrire

Students choose from among the following four written scenarios:

 Journal This weekend you visited a place you've always wanted to see. Write a journal entry telling what you did and what and whom you saw.

 E-mail Write a series of e-mail messages between two friends. One friend has a problem at school. He or she asks for help, explains the problem, and thanks the other friend, who offers help and gives advice.

 Note You've just received a note from your best friend, who's met someone he or she is interested in. Your friend is asking for advice on how to ask this person out. Write a note back.

 Letter Write a letter to the Tourist Office in Arles and tell them about your visit to their city. Tell what you did and saw, and what you liked and didn't like.

Dans un magasin de vêtements

Guided Recording

A toi de parler

Students record a conversation with a partner based on the following prompts:

CUSTOMER Get the salesperson's attention and say that you're looking for a sweater in a specific color of your choice.

SALESPERSON Tell the customer that you have a sweater in that color.

CUSTOMER Ask if you can try it on in a certain size.

SALESPERSON Tell your customer he or she can try it on, and then compliment your customer on how the sweater looks. Ask if he or she will take it.

CUSTOMER Tell the salesperson that you like the sweater and you'll take it.

SALESPERSON Give the price of the sweater and thank your customer.

Guided Writing

A toi d'écrire

Students choose from among the following four writing scenarios:

 Survey Create a six-to-eight question survey asking your classmates about their favorite clothes and accessories. You may want to ask about the color and fit of the items.

 Conversation Create an eight-to-ten line conversation between a salesperson and a customer who can't find anything that fits. The customer should ask to try on two or three items of clothing, and the salesperson should comment on the fit and style of each.

 Note Write a note to your friends, Sophie and Eric, suggesting an outfit for each one to wear to a wedding next weekend. Explain why you think these outfits are good choices.

 Advertisement Create an advertisement for two or three articles of clothing. Be sure to tell what colors the items come in and how much they cost. Create slogans to help persuade people to buy these items. You may want to leave space to add illustrations after you have printed out your advertisement.

CD-ROM ASSESSMENT

Vive les vacances!

Guided Recording

A toi de parler

Students record a conversation based on the following video prompts:

1. J'ai passé des vacances formidables! Et toi, tu as passé un bon été?
2. Tu es allé(e) où?
3. Tu y es allé(e) avec qui?
4. Qu'est-ce que tu as fait là-bas?
5. C'était comment?

Guided Writing

A toi d'écrire

Students choose from among the following four writing scenarios:

 Letter You've just returned home after a really bad vacation. Write a letter to your pen pal, Bruno, telling him about the weather, two or three things you did, and how you felt about everything.

 Conversation Create an eight-to-ten-line conversation in which a travel agent is helping a client plan a vacation. Before suggesting a destination, the travel agent should find out what the client likes to do and to what kind of place he or she wants to go.

 Note You're interested in your friend Claire's travel plans. Write her a note in which you ask where she's going and what she's going to do. Remind her of at least two specific items she should not forget.

 Advertisement Create a travel brochure for your hometown or another place of your choice. Tell about the weather and what there is to see and do there. You may wish to leave space to add illustrations after you print out your brochure.

12 En ville

Guided Recording

A toi de parler

Students record a conversation based on the following video prompts:

1. Tu sais, je vais aller en ville faire des courses. Est-ce qu'il te faut quelque chose?
2. D'accord. Où est-ce que je dois aller?
3. C'est loin d'ici? Je prends le bus ou j'y vais à pied?
4. C'est dans quelle direction? Comment j'y vais?
5. Bon. C'est tout? Il te faut autre chose?

Guided Writing

A toi d'écrire

Students choose from among the following four writing scenarios.

 Note Write a note asking a friend to run three or four errands for you. Give the location of or directions to any specific places you ask your friend to go to. Explain why you can't run the errands yourself.

 List Create a list of six or seven of the places you learned in this chapter. Then list at least three items you can buy, or three errands you can run at each place. You may wish to mention items you learned about in previous chapters.

 Conversation Create an eight-to-ten-line conversation between a tourist who's looking for at least three specific places and a person giving him or her directions.

 Letter Write a letter to a friend telling him or her about the great trip you had to Martinique. Use the Process Writing steps below to complete your letter.

PROCESS WRITING steps for **Letter** assignment

PREWRITING Brainstorm a list of the places you went to and tell what you did at each place.

WRITING Select four or five of the places from your PREWRITING list and write a two-to-three-sentence paragraph explaining what you did at each location. Give your opinion of each place. You should also include information about how you traveled from place to place.

REVISING Print out your letter, make any necessary changes to improve it, and check it for correct spelling, accents, and capitalization.

PUBLISHING Correct any errors, rewrite anything you need to for greater clarity or emphasis, and print out a copy of your finished letter.
